THE GROWTH AND NATURE OF
EGYPTOLOGY

T0349859

THE GROWTH AND NATURE OF
EGYPTOLOGY

AN INAUGURAL LECTURE

BY

S. R. K. GLANVILLE

Herbert Thompson Professor of Egyptology
in the University of Cambridge

CAMBRIDGE
AT THE UNIVERSITY PRESS
1947

CAMBRIDGE
UNIVERSITY PRESS

University Printing House, Cambridge CB2 8BS, United Kingdom

Published in the United States of America by Cambridge University Press, New York

Cambridge University Press is part of the University of Cambridge.

It furthers the University's mission by disseminating knowledge in the pursuit of education, learning and research at the highest international levels of excellence.

www.cambridge.org
Information on this title: www.cambridge.org/9781107637771

© Cambridge University Press 1947

First published 1947
First paperback edition 2014

A catalogue record for this publication is available from the British Library

ISBN 978-1-107-63777-1 Paperback

IT MAY BE ASSUMED, I suppose, that no University in this country would to-day create a new Chair which it did not consider met a need, however limited. But if I therefore take for granted your charitable welcome to a Professorship of Egyptology at Cambridge, I realize too that you may wish to know what contribution the subject can make to university education as a whole, and perhaps even what Egyptology really is. For it is true that it is possible to spend a lifetime without having meditated upon the content of that word and be none the worse for it. Not that I wish to be too modest on behalf of my subject. 'Egyptian history', wrote Wilkinson ninety years ago, 'Egyptian history and the manners of one of the most ancient nations, cannot but be interesting to every one.'

Nor, on the other hand, is it in any aggressive spirit that I call your attention to an apparent tardiness on the part of this University in giving due recognition to Egyptology. The subject has a certain claim to antiquity. London first gave it academic standing in this country with the foundation fifty-five years ago of the Edwards Professorship at University College for Flinders Petrie. Oxford followed in 1901 with a two-term Readership whose first holder, F. Ll. Griffith, brought it such distinction that he was later given the title of Professor and a full Chair was created for his successor. Liverpool came next with a Professorship in 1906; and from 1912–14 Manchester had a Readership, although since then the teaching of Egyptology in that University has been provided by the Professor at Liverpool. Thus, in the space of thirty years, Egyptologists were installed at four of our Universities—Universities of very different traditions. Cambridge has waited all but another quarter of a century to follow suit. The explanation of the delay is probably not merely that Cambridge had to wait for a benefactor, as London and Liverpool had to. The truth is that Egyptology is never likely to be able to claim anything but a modest place in the academic economy. But that it has its place, if only a modest place, I hope to be able to persuade you this afternoon.

Before I come to that theme, let me try and make amends for any stricture which may seem to have been implied in the statistics I have just given. Cambridge, without a school of Egyptology, has produced her great Egyptologists. Three names stand out.

The least familiar to-day, but the greatest intellect among them and the one for whom it may properly be claimed that he was a pioneer in the subject, was CHARLES WYCLIFFE GOODWIN. Born in 1817, the son of a King's Lynn solicitor, he came up to St Catharine's and graduated, in 1838, 6th Classic and senior optime in Mathematics. After three leisurely

6

years, spent visiting friends, he read for the Bar at Lincoln's Inn and was called in 1843. Finding the Law uncongenial, he returned to Cambridge the following year with a Fellowship at his old College, having still in mind an earlier intention to take Holy Orders, and determined to teach. Within a year or two he resigned his Fellowship on the ground that he could no longer conscientiously accept all the doctrines of the Church, and went back to London to practise as a barrister. So he continued till 1865, when he was appointed Assistant Judge for the Supreme Court for China and Japan, married, and removed to Shanghai. There he remained (except for a single visit to England on leave) till his death in 1878, having succeeded to the Chief Judgeship two years earlier.

By the time Goodwin finally left Cambridge, he was a first-class Greek scholar, an accomplished Hebraist, and an authority on Anglo-Saxon with valuable editions of new texts to his credit. He also had a considerable knowledge of natural history, especially geology. In London, where his practice was not large, he wrote music and art criticism; was for a time editor of the *Literary Gazette*; was the only layman among the seven contributors to the much talked of *Essays and Reviews* (1860); and, because of his Greek and Hebrew scholarship, was frequently consulted by the Revisers of the New Testament. But throughout his life his main interest, begun when he

7

was at school, was in the elucidation of Ancient Egyptian and Coptic texts, more especially those Egyptian texts written in the cursive script called hieratic.

In London he spent much of his time in the British Museum, copying papyri. He was in close touch with Samuel Birch, then Keeper of the Oriental Department, and was constantly exchanging information by correspondence with the other leading Egyptologists of his day. He was indeed accepted as one of their number, and his biographer[1] has remarked that when Sir Henry Layard as Parliamentary Under-Secretary to Earl Russell, then Foreign Minister, forwarded Goodwin's application for a legal appointment in the East, he made no reference to Goodwin's legal qualifications, but pressed the claim of his scholarship and especially of his study of hieratic papyri; and when, a few years later, a friend wrote to Lord Granville at the Foreign Office, suggesting that Goodwin (against the latter's own wishes) should be found a post in Egypt, Granville replied: 'His eminence as an Egyptological discoverer is well known, and I should be very glad if it were in my power to afford him an opportunity of further advancing the important science which already owes so much to his energy and critical insight.'

---

[1] Warren R. Dawson, on whose monograph, *Charles Wycliffe Goodwin*, 1817–1878. *A Pioneer in Egyptology*, Oxford University Press, 1934, this account is based.

Goodwin published a very considerable number of short articles on his Egyptian studies, mostly in foreign journals, which reveal not only his intellectual power, but also the capital importance of his contribution to the development of Egyptological research in his day. But his reputation in the science would have been made by, and would stand for all time on, his essay 'Hieratic Papyri', published in 1858 in *Cambridge Essays*. In this, to quote his biographer, 'Goodwin shows himself to be at once a skilled decipherer of hieratic writing and a brilliant interpreter of it'. It was the foundation on which most subsequent translators of these documents built, and has rightly been called in our own day epoch-making.

I have spoken at some length of C. W. Goodwin, but I hope you will agree that this is a fitting place in which to pay tribute to that one of the small band of Egyptological pioneers who owed the greater part of his training for scholarship to Cambridge. I will speak more briefly of the other two to whom I have referred.

Goodwin had been indefatigable in his correspondence on Egyptian subjects with Sir Peter le Page Renouf who succeeded Birch at the British Museum in 1885. Two years earlier, E. A. WALLIS BUDGE had joined the Department as an assistant. Budge had studied cuneiform in the early days of its decipherment and was sent up to Christ's at Mr Gladstone's suggestion to read Oriental Languages under William Wright. His early work in the Museum was devoted to Assyrian texts, but for official reasons Birch directed him to hieroglyphic studies, which he had begun years before. On Renouf's retirement in 1892 Budge was made Acting Keeper, and Keeper in 1894. By the time he retired in 1924, he could show a list of publications, both technical and popular, unrivalled in bulk and in range of subject by those of any other Egyptologist; he had been responsible for securing large and valuable increases to the collections in his Department, notably in the field of papyri; he had produced, with the help of his staff, the most instructive set of *Guides* to be found in any Department in the Museum, and had maintained at high pressure the principle that a primary obligation of the Museum's officers was to publish the material—whether papyri, tablets, or antiquities—for which they were responsible to the public. He received a knighthood in recognition of his vigorous and single-purposed devotion to the safety of the collections under his charge during the War of 1914–18. By his popular books Budge made a small public as familiar with Egyptian writing, literature, and thought, as Sir Flinders Petrie made it familiar with Egyptian archaeology, long before the discovery of the Tomb of Tutankhamen and an enlightened management of the *Illustrated London News* had made the whole of the literate population excavation-conscious.

Popular writing on such a scale by a scholar easily invites criticism from academic colleagues; so prolific an output of learned books could only be achieved at some cost in accuracy; so single-minded a loyalty to what he conceived to be his duty to the nation, as represented by the Trustees of the Museum, inevitably brought him into conflict with individuals outside it. Probably no Egyptologist of his stature—which none could deny him—enjoyed a worse reputation among his colleagues than did Budge at the height of his power and productivity. After his retirement many old animosities were dissipated. When he died in 1934, a memorial service at St Paul's brought together most of the Egyptologists in the country, among them some of his bitterest critics. It was a tribute, grudging perhaps, to a giant. By his will he divided his estate between University College, Oxford, and his old College at Cambridge, to provide at each institution an Egyptological foundation to be named after his wife. To Christ's also he left his library.

I think it is beyond question that Wallis Budge did more than any other man to rouse in the ordinary reader of this country an interest in the language and writings of Ancient Egypt. The splendid volumes of facsimiles of papyri which he edited for the British Museum, often with transliterations and translations, together with a certain number of his own editions of texts, both Ancient Egyptian and Coptic, are indispensable to-day and will remain so for many years; and to Cambridge he gave her first Egyptological foundation. He, too, should be remembered gratefully and with pride on this occasion.[1]

I pass to the third name, that of SIR HERBERT THOMPSON, to whose benefaction to the University I owe it that I am speaking here now. He was born in 1859—only two years after Wallis Budge—and left Marlborough at the age of sixteen, having reached the top of the school and won a major scholarship at Trinity. After a year in Germany and some months in a London business office, he came up to Cambridge, but failed to distinguish himself in the Classical Tripos, apparently from over-study—a not common cause. At his father's wish he read for the Bar, was called, and practised for some years in the chambers of the late W. O. Danckwerts. But, though his legal experience was to be of great value to him in his Demotic work later on, practising in the Courts was entirely uncongenial. (His real interest at this time was in music and art, medieval studies, Icelandic— and always the classics.) His father agreed to his giving up the Bar on condition that he took up Biology. This new career proved abortive; too strenuous use of the microscope seriously damaged his

[1] The earliest Egyptian collections in the Fitzwilliam Museum owed much to Budge; and an *Introduction* which he planned to his *Catalogue* of the Collection grew into *The Mummy*, in its second and much enlarged edition (Cambridge University Press, 1925) still perhaps the best general handbook on Egyptology.

sight, and for some months he was unable to use his eyes. His vision was saved, but the microscope was forbidden. The accident of proximity to Flinders Petrie led to his taking up Egyptology at University College, London, at the age of forty. F. Ll. Griffith and W. E. Crum were teaching at University College at this time and under their influence Thompson came to confine himself to Demotic and Coptic after a preliminary training in the earlier stages of the language. When he died, forty-five years later, he was the leading Demotist of his day and among the first three or four Copticists.

If you look up the entry against Henry Francis Herbert Thompson in a volume of *Who's Who* for the early 1940's, you will find it comprised in seven or eight lines. There is no reference to the remarkable musician, Kate Fanny Loder, his mother, devotion to whose memory was one of the reasons for his retirement to her native town of Bath; no mention of the six or seven major publications of texts which will perpetuate his memory. This extreme reticence and modesty were to the ordinary observer the most characteristic marks of the man; though they could not entirely conceal his extraordinary generosity from his friends. Nothing would have more distressed him than to know that an encomium on himself was to be delivered in public. I have written elsewhere more than he would have cared to read about himself. Adequately to record my own debt to him as teacher and friend would be quite outside the scope of this lecture. To-day I ask you to be content with this bare witness to his distinction as a scholar.

I think I have said enough to show that Cambridge had already made a worthy contribution to Egyptology before the subject had any place in the University's curriculum. It must suffice only to mention some later names: among my seniors when I first came to the subject, two archaeologists, J. E. Quibell and F. W. Green, and two Copticists, Forbes Robertson and Stephen Gaselee; among contemporaries, Sidney Smith (Budge's second successor) and I. E. S. Edwards at the British Museum, and two who died in action in the recent war, John Pendlebury on his way to becoming an archaeological colossus with one foot in Crete and the other in Egypt, and Charles Allberry who at one blow had established his reputation as a Coptic scholar in the first class. Were he alive to-day, Cambridge would have had no need to import her first Herbert Thompson Professor.

But to return to the progress and nature of Egyptology. As a scientific study Egyptology is a comparatively modern development—the latest arrival among the Humanities. This is not entirely due to lack of material to work upon, and certainly not to lack of interest. There is ample testimony in the classical writers not only to contemporary curiosity about the earlier and, as they recognized, long-lived history of the Egyptians, but also to the importance of its contribution to civilization; and this tradition was to some extent revived with the recovery of Greek and Latin texts after the Renaissance. But by that time the key to any fundamental study—ability to read Egyptian hieroglyphic writing—was lost, and sources available to any would-be student virtually confined to the standing monuments of Egypt, which were almost inaccessible to Europeans, and to a small number of obelisks which had been transported to Rome or Constantinople by Trajan and others. These did, indeed, provoke some attempts at decipherment which, however, were almost entirely without success, because the phonetic character of the writing had not been recognized. The accounts brought back from Egypt by occasional European visitors during the seventeenth and eighteenth centuries could add very little to what was known from the classics.

It was not till Napoleon commissioned, at the end of the eighteenth century, a scientific expedition— the savants who provoked the soldierly witticisms of his grenadiers—to record observable data about the country ancient and modern, that material in any quantity became available for study; nor till Champollion had published in 1822 his account of the principle of the writing, together with the first hieroglyphic alphabet, that the discipline which we now call Egyptology was born. Its coming of age, its recognition by the learned world, was naturally a good deal later; let us say about 1860, a year after the earliest use of the word recorded by the *New English Dictionary* and three years after the Khedive Ismail had made official recognition of Egypt's responsibility for the recovery and preservation of her antiquities by appointing Auguste Mariette as Director of Antiquity Works, the forerunner of the present Department of Antiquities.

The progress achieved by that date was impressive, but it was the progress of a child whose lurching steps carry it further in the direction of the first stride than it intends, covering a good deal of ground to right and left with comparatively little forward movement. On the one hand a too narrow concentration on philological research was indifferent to the fate of antiquities and thus neglected evidence outside its own immediate purpose. On the other a preoccupation with the recovery of antiquities as so much treasure-trove, chiefly for the enhancement of the large European museums and the satisfaction of an uninstructed public curiosity, destroyed almost as much evidence as it garnered. We may perhaps see an intermediate way in that pursued by the small band of English copyists, Hay, Burton and J. G. Wilkinson, which culminated in the latter's *Manners and Customs of the Ancient Egyptians*. Published over a century ago, it was for more than half that time the standard work in its field; and some of the drawings of scenes from temples and tombs by these three pioneers are still of value to-day.

Mariette's insistence on the central control of excavation—and the work he himself carried out up and down Egypt—marked a great advance; but full appreciation of the part that could be played by archaeological field work and the interpretation of antiquities, if archaeology and philology were to achieve a satisfactory combination, began only with the arrival of Flinders Petrie at the Pyramids in 1880 and his first excavations in the years that immediately followed.

The last sixty-five years have reinforced the foundations, identified and strengthened the structural elements, and supplied an intelligible 'architect's drawing' of the whole Egyptological edifice. We have reached the point where we can begin to think of completing the brickwork and plastering, consider the final appearance of the façade and even plan the internal decoration. We have come a long way in less than a century and a half, but others have also been building in our intellectual city, and our viewpoint has begun to change. We are now beginning to be less preoccupied with building an Egyptological home. We are becoming more and more concerned with our relations with our neighbours of Assyriology, Papyrology, Theology, and the like—in a word with our place in the community of ancient historians. But let us first look at our architect's plans.

The *New English Dictionary* defines 'Egyptologist' as 'One versed in the study of Egyptian antiquities'.

The definition is, I think, quite inadequate to-day; but it is significant because it clearly indicates the centripetal emphasis that has controlled our study for the greater part of its history. The concrete term 'antiquities' suggests, too, the reason why the study lacked for so long a synthesizing force. If we examine the nature of these antiquities, we find that they fall into three roughly defined categories: First there are the monuments standing above ground in Egypt to-day, temples, tombs, colossal statues, obelisks, sphinxes, stelae. All these—apart from their architectural and religious functions—have one common characteristic; they are all almost without exception engraved or painted with hieroglyphic writing or with pictorial scenes, or indeed both. To these must be added a much smaller number of mud-brick buildings, for the most part unpainted and uninscribed, of which the essential interest is therefore architectural; and that relatively small part, but yet considerable total of stone monuments of the kind just referred to, which have been removed to other countries—the obelisks slowly perishing from exposure to the climate and smoke of modern capitals, a few whole mastaba tombs of the Old Kingdom, columns, altars, door-jambs, lintels and colossal statues, and a large number of stelae from temples or (much more often) from tombs—all in museums. For convenience I will refer to this category as 'Monuments'.

The second category of antiquities includes the

whole range of sculpture, from life-size monolithic figures to small stone statuettes, derived from temples and tombs, as well as that great majority of Egyptian antiquities representative of every aspect of life and death and made of every material known to the Egyptians, which were, with very few exceptions, once the contents of tombs, whether rock-hewn vaults or shallow desert pits—coffins, furniture, jewellery, tools, weapons, and utensils of stone and pottery. Inscriptions are to be found on a large number of these objects, but a very much greater number have none. As a class, much more is to be learnt from them and about them from their intrinsic nature and from their archaeological associations than from the inscriptions some of them bear, and as a class they all eventually find their way to museums or—a very small minority—to private collections. Finally, they are abundantly the most numerous of the three categories. Let me speak of them as 'Antiquities', remembering that we are using the word for the time being in a deliberately restricted sense.

The third category comprises papyri and ostraca, and a few documents on other materials, e.g. leather, vellum, parchment and wooden boards with or without a plaster surface. Their interest lies entirely in the writing they bear, the character of the script, the language it expresses, and, above all, the story it has to tell. They, too, are as good as non-existent till they reach museums or—rarely nowadays—the collector's hands. I will refer to them for short as 'Papyri, etc.'

But if almost all 'Antiquities' and 'Papyri' now have their homes in museums, there is one important distinction to be made between them: whereas the papyri, leather rolls, tablets, etc.—to a lesser extent ostraca—have usually reached the students' hands by way of dealers or early collectors and thus have no known provenance, enough examples of almost every class of object included under 'Antiquities' have now been recovered by scientific excavation to provide a great deal more knowledge about any individual object than could be deduced from mere observation and study of the object itself. There are, in fact, very few kinds of Egyptian antiquities of whose original function we are ignorant to-day, and in many cases the information obtained from their archaeological association, mainly as deduced from excavations, but also as illustrated by temple or tomb scenes, is of more value for the understanding of larger issues, e.g. chronology, religious beliefs or social customs, than for our knowledge of the nature of the objects themselves.

Now this distinction between 'Antiquities' and 'Papyri, etc.' as material for study in the museum is of little consequence to-day. Often what we lose on the swings, we gain on the roundabouts; a papyrus of whose origin nothing at all is known before it is studied in the museum may reveal by internal evidence its original association with a well-known tomb, a site, or another group of documents, or an excavation. It was very different in those pioneering second and third quarters of the last century. The museums had already amassed considerable collections of objects from Egypt, but Petrie had not yet demonstrated to Egyptologists what is an archaeological commonplace of to-day, namely that the key to extracting their story from antiquities lies in exact observation and interpretation during excavation. The papyri then had so much more information to offer, and so much study was obviously still required to recover that information from them, that the serious student of Ancient Egypt inevitably tended to neglect what I have called 'Antiquities' in the narrower sense. Thus was intensified a dichotomy of interest which had arisen partly through circumstance, partly through natural attraction and aptitude for archaeological or philological study respectively.

You will have realized from this very rough classification of the material presented to the Egyptologist that certain lines of inquiry were plainly indicated to the early student. Thus the monuments immediately produced a body of evidence about Egyptian architecture. Sculpture in the round, on the other hand, which was represented mainly by colossal figures and sphinxes and was divided between the monuments *in situ* and the comparatively small number of statues in museums, naturally took a second place; and indeed it is only in the last twenty or thirty years that Egyptian art as a whole has begun to receive the study and appreciation it deserves.

The monuments also supplied the bulk of hiero-glyphic writing, and since this was an integral part of the temples, tombs and statues on which it was carved or painted, and since behind all these lay a religious conception, the bulk of hieroglyphic writing had a religious content, often of course in addition to a political or biographical content. Practically all inscribed material in museums (other than papyri, etc.) consisted of stelae and architectural fragments, and thus formed a part of the same corpus of hiero-glyphic texts. Finally, the great majority of papyri (but excluding ostraca) were purely religious texts for the use of the dead, and a large part of these—and these only—were written in a linear script, easily recognizable as hieroglyphic; whereas all literary texts (as well as some religious) were written in a cursive script derived from hieroglyphs, which added an initial problem of decipherment to that of under-standing the language now becoming intelligible in its hieroglyphic form. (And it might be added that among the antiquities in museums a prominent class was the large range of figures representing gods and goddesses in human or animal form.) Thus, inevitably, the ancient religion became a main field of study for the early Egyptologists.

A less extensive—though to-day much increased—

feature of the monuments was the variety of stereo-typed scenes from daily life preserved on tomb walls. These were being exploited by the copyists, mainly at Thebes and, later, in the Pyramid area, from the beginning of the last century. They provided, in anticipation of excavation, a commentary on the antiquities in museums, and the antiquities in turn assisted the interpretation of drawings in an unfamiliar artistic convention. From this interaction, but based primarily on the tomb paintings, came Wilkinson's *Manners and Customs* already referred to. It was the beginning of a branch of Egyptian studies which tended to become more specialized as its importance for every kind of Egyptological activity was realized, and which achieved in the hands of the small band of modern copyists, who have made it their main concern, a scholarly and artistic excellence which seems final. In the process the emphasis has shifted from the content of the scenes depicted to the quality and manner of their execution. Reproductions of paintings and reliefs have supplied the main evidence for the study of Egyptian art as an entity independent of its archaeological or historical associations, an achievement which will bear comparison with the other great artistic movements in human history.

You will already have noticed that, though each category of antiquities tends to initiate or emphasize certain fields of Egyptian studies, these studies are not confined to one or another category. The analysis by

23

categories was an artificial device, useful for displaying the historical development of Egyptology, but meaningless, or almost so—it should be entirely —for the modern student. This first becomes obvious when we look more closely at the part played by the language. The language, in whatever form—and of that more in a moment—is the key in greater or lesser extent to the understanding of all categories of Egyptian antiquities. It is the flux by means of which the information derived from different categories can be fused into a single account.

Thus, detailed study of architectural forms enables us to guess pretty accurately the relative chronological order of Pyramids or *Mastaba*-tombs and to assign them to their respective periods or even dynasties, but only the written word will pin-point them to their precise place in the dynasty and tie them up with relevant information from other sources. Careful excavation will provide a group of associations among whole ranges of antiquities and reveal a consistent and trustworthy archaeological pattern; but this pattern may be moved about like an isolated group of pieces in the centre of a jig-saw puzzle until anchored by an inscription to the more rigid framework of history. The general character of scenes on temple walls or in tomb paintings and reliefs is immediately clear to the beholder, but only the accompanying hieroglyphs turn generalizations into historical records, explain the ceremonial purpose of a gesture, or define the action of a craftsman at work. The most significant detail about a work of art *may* be the traces of a name that has been intentionally, but incompletely erased.

Writing is first found in Egypt a century or two before 3000 B.C., consisting of small groups of hiero-glyphs, for the most part on clay seal-impressions, on ivory and wooden tablets, and on stone vases. This picture writing, greatly enriched, was still in use in the fourth century A.D. Under the influence of the writing hand, using pen and ink, the hieroglyphs, which were retained throughout the whole period for epigraphic purposes, were gradually reduced to cursive forms, in which two systems are clearly distin-guished, the one (demotic) being a further reduction from the other (hieratic). At the beginning of our era all three forms of writing were concurrently in use for different purposes. These are partly reflected in the Greek names by which they are still distin-guished: hieroglyphic, the sacred, because God-given, original form of the writing, confined to epigraphy, whether in temple or tomb; hieratic, used by this time only for religious books; and demotic, the writing for all secular purposes (but also occasionally for religious works and even for inscriptions)—the ordinary current hand of the day in fact. The evolu-tion of hieratic from hieroglyphic and of demotic from hieratic is clearly demonstrable, and each system can show its own development over a long period—a thousand years even for demotic which began at about 650 B.C. The essential character of the Egyptian hieroglyphic writing, namely that it is a combination of phonetic and ideographic signs, was retained in the cursive systems.

It is axiomatic that an unknown language in an unknown script cannot be safely interpreted without a bilingual text. For Egyptian the Rosetta Stone provided this basis, giving an inscription in Greek, hieroglyphic and demotic. Three or four more inscriptions, also of the Ptolemaic period, complete our bilingual resources. But there was also Coptic which preserved, within its narrow scope, the latest phase of Ancient Egyptian in Greek script, and has never ceased to be used in the Christian Churches of Egypt. Though by itself it had proved useless as a means to reading the *writing*, once the bilingual inscription had yielded its clue, Coptic immediately became an all-important aid to the understanding of the *language*. The task for the Egyptologist, then, was to extend his ability to read and understand a limited range of Ptolemaic hieroglyphs backwards over a period of 3000 years.

The next step was to attack the cursive systems, starting at one end of the time-scale with the hieratic literary hands whose form showed a recognizable approximation to hieroglyphic, and at the other end with demotic for which a nucleus of hieroglyphic equivalents (with their Greek meanings) was available in the trilingual and bilingual inscriptions already mentioned. Some of the documentary hands in hieratic, both earlier and later, are, as one would expect, of a more cursive character than those used in writing literary texts; papyri employing these, notably certain classes of accounts and legal documents, still present sufficient difficulty to the decipherer to require a degree of specialization which relegates them to the care of a handful of scholars. By the time that demotic had reached what may be called its classical stage, in the Ptolemaic period, cursive writing had developed so far from its hieroglyphic original that, generally speaking, only an historical connection was left between the two scripts. The demotic scribe was not conscious of writing abbreviated hieroglyphs, and as a rule was probably unable to read the hieroglyphic inscriptions which he might see whenever he visited the temples. Similarly, for the modern student, the reading of a demotic text requires him to think in terms of that script alone and to recognize the phonetic values of the words as they are written; though the fact that he is equipped with a better knowledge of the earlier phases of the writing and of the language than was the writer of his text, to some extent offsets his disadvantage, as compared with the latter, in understanding the meaning of the words he can read. The combination, however, of the different kinds of hieroglyphic signs, ideographic and phonetic, still underlies demotic writing, with the result that what might have been a very simple script is a highly complicated one, requiring continuous application for its decipherment. Partly for this reason it too tends to be the field of a few specialists.

Nevertheless, it may be said that to-day there is no Ancient Egyptian writing that cannot be read, with the exception of odd words here and there, and a few isolated signs whose meaning is clear, but whose reading is still unknown or uncertain. The present position of our understanding of the Ancient Egyptian language is more complicated and less satisfactory than our capacity to read the writing of it.

Egyptologists distinguish four separate phases of the written language before Coptic: Old, Middle and Late Egyptian, and Demotic. This is by no means an entirely artificial classification: though the change is gradual from phase to phase, each is marked by its own grammar, vocabulary, and—though here with greater variability—orthography. In their study of grammar and orthography alike, Egyptologists have reached, or are in process of reaching, something like definitive standards. Progress in our knowledge of the meaning of words and of the historical development of the language is slower, partly because we are dealing with a dead language for which Coptic provides clues only to a very limited range of the vocabulary, partly for reasons which are inherent in the character of the writing. It might be supposed that a method of writing, which included in the spelling of the great majority of words an ideogram giving some indication of the general sense of the word, would be of great assistance to the modern lexicographer. And so indeed it is; but the ideograms necessarily provide only a generic meaning—a *kind* of plant, a *kind* of receptacle, the *idea of abstraction* for instance. These admittedly tell us something, yet they have had at the same time the unfortunate result of beguiling us into being apt to think we are nearer the meaning than in fact we are. Only too often the standard dictionaries are content with just such a generic definition as I quoted a moment ago. The main hindrance to a full understanding of Egyptian texts is the vagueness of our vocabulary, and the prime need of Egyptian philology to-day is more thorough lexicographical study. This, by the collation of all known contexts, like that which for centuries has been applied to Greek and Latin, will give us more precise meanings for many common words in our texts, as well as for hundreds which are comparatively rare.

In the study of the grammar and especially in attempting to trace the development of the language through its consecutive stages, we are faced with the difficulty that Egyptian orthography disregarded vowels. Since Ancient Egyptian was an inflected language, this means that many different forms of the same word (not to mention different words spelt with the same consonants in the same order) are indistinguishable in the writing. Here Coptic, aided by general phonetic laws and an examination of the orthographic changes exhibited by the several phases of the language, is gradually enabling us to build a foundation of philological fact; but much remains to be done and, in default of a good deal more material than we at present possess, it looks as if there must be a strict limitation to further progress. Even so, this is not perhaps, as you will shortly see, the most serious disadvantage which we suffer from the omission of vowels in the Egyptian writing.

If I have digressed at too great length on the writing and language of Ancient Egypt, my excuse is that the Herbert Thompson Chair is, by the terms of its foundation, primarily concerned with the study of Demotic and Coptic; and of the wider interests of these two studies I shall have a little more to say later. Yet it was a digression from the point that I was trying to make, that the written word is an essential tool in the investigation of almost every aspect of Ancient Egyptian civilization. And, although, as we have just seen, there is ample work to be done in the purely philological field for those who are attracted by it alone, the main function of linguistic research is, in my view, to be ancillary to a larger field of study.

First—this hardly needs saying—comes literature. It has to be confessed that, considering the immense quantity of Ancient Egyptian writing of all kinds which are available for reading to-day, the total body of what by any reasonable criterion can be called literature that has survived, and been recovered—as opposed to what may still await excavation—is small enough. Yet it can, I think, be demonstrated that the selection we possess of short stories, sacred and profane poetry, hymns, satire and wisdom literature are only the mere samples of a grand tradition. A more serious limitation to our evaluation of Egyptian literature which must be accepted—though I do not think it always is—is the difficulty, I am inclined to say impossibility, of really appreciating as literature texts in which you can only guess at the quality and quantity of the vowel sounds and even at the position of those vowels in their consonantal skeletons, and in which you are constantly unaware of the nuances of words or even sometimes of their meaning. Finally, the difficulty of appreciation has been increased in the past by a tendency among Egyptologists to render Egyptian into an archaic English modelled on the Authorized Version. This at best obscures the atmosphere by a false association, at worst is manifestly inconsistent with the character and style of the text, and for obvious reasons is in any case almost certainly doomed to failure. Despite these limitations it is possible to distinguish in Egyptian literature broad differentiations of style; to appreciate the straightforward economy of some narrative and the comparative wealth of vocabulary in others; to discern the beauty or aptness of images in prose as well as poetry and to share the pathos and the joy of many of the songs and hymns.

The language is also the main key to the sciences; to mathematics on which we have unfortunately only two major papyri; to astronomy; to metrology—though here archaeological evidence plays at least as great a part; to medicine with which must be included magic; to geography which leads us, by its intimate connection, to history.

The clue to the decipherment of the Egyptian inscriptions on the Rosetta-stone was the guess that the 'cartouches'—the oval outlines which we now know normally surround royal names in hieroglyphic writing—contained the name of Ptolemy, which occurred in the parallel Greek text, coupled with the assumption that, since this was a foreign name, it must be written phonetically in Egyptian. The phonetic values thus obtained were then applied to other words in the Egyptian which might be assumed to correspond from their position with words in the Greek text and of which the Coptic equivalents were known. Thus, symbolically, the decipherment of Egyptian and the whole study of Egyptology grew out of the reading of royal cartouches. Immediately the monuments were ransacked for cartouches and the hieroglyphic forms of new kings' names identified. From the beginning of scientific Egyptology, the recovery of the history of the country became not only a main focus of study, but the framework into which every contributory fact about Egyptian civilization was keyed. The old definition of Egyptology: 'the Study of Egyptian Antiquities' is thus quite inadequate; Egyptology is 'the study of the history of the Ancient Egyptian civilization'. For that study the Egyptian language must inevitably be the most fruitful source. It provides regnal dates and genealogies, the bones of a chronological skeleton; official records, royal decrees and the biographies of the great, the outline of the historical body; letters, accounts, and legal documents to fill in the anatomy. But with the language as our only source we should be left with a two-dimensional sketch, a diagram for the class-room wall.

It is here that archaeology comes to the rescue, checking and refining chronological calculations, filling in the detail of pharaonic activities at home and abroad, defining artistic standards and official standing, but above all illustrating the background of social and economic life and providing a concrete continuum which converts the diagram into a tangible figure. Of no other people in antiquity have we such a rich and variegated material documentation.

And yet this massive portrait, offering us at once details of the lives of thousands of private individuals and the very bodies of kings, illustrations of every craft and agricultural activity, official accounts of imperial conquest, of booty brought home from the wars or of lions taken in a local hunt, crown jewels and paupers' trinkets—this is not history as we know it. It is not what we mean by history when we think of modern history or medieval history, or even ancient history when by that term is understood the history of Greece and Rome. Egyptian history lacks a living principle; once again we are faced with a seemingly ineluctable limitation inherent in the nature of our subject.

It is not, I think, difficult to see the cause of this limitation. Despite the innate conservatism of the race and the obsession of individuals, from Pharaoh to the humblest of his subjects who could afford a funerary inscription, to secure a memorial with posterity, the Egyptians had no instinct for history. Their first historian was a foreigner, writing of them as their sun declined (but still with an unquestioning respect) whom we significantly call the Father of History. Out of a remarkable, but as yet imperfectly understood, period of internal upheaval towards the end of the third millennium come one or two texts whose authors recorded the stress of the times they lived in; but these are the lamentations of prophets or politicians, not the witness of historians, and even so they stand alone. And it is not an exaggeration to say that no single individual in Egyptian history, known to us from the inscriptions, is able to convey to us the quality of his personality. As a nation and as individuals the Egyptians were fundamentally

34

conventional; aiming in their biographies at respectability above all else, in their official records at propaganda, and expressing both in clichés. It seems highly improbable that the most patient and prolonged study of their almost unlimited remains will ever enable us to do for them what they did not seek to do for themselves, and that is to write their history. For the moment we must admit that historiography was not born when the Egyptians were splendidly making history.

We are now within sight of a final evaluation of Egyptology. We have observed its inherent limitations; but we have not looked outside it for factors which may limit or extend its significance. The Egyptians, like other nations, who have enjoyed a predominant position among their contemporaries, were at least sufficiently self-conscious to think of themselves as a chosen people, and of their neighbours as barbarians, a species of human being different in kind. They were not by nature aggressive in the modern sense of the word, and for essential commodities they were economically self-sufficient. Yet from before historic times they were culturally and economically in contact with the peoples surrounding them, and it is becoming increasingly clear that our best hope of a greater understanding of Egyptian history lies in closer study of the cultural and economic factors underlying Egypt's foreign relations, and in recognizing those habits of mind which seemed to

35

have been the common inheritance of the whole civilized world at given stages of antiquity. For we see now that the geographical unit of pre-classical Ancient History is a single area, Egypt and Western Asia and the Eastern Mediterranean; and that the primary subdivisions of this unit are chronological cross-sections of the whole, within which further subdivisions by countries may then be made. Thus, though the history of Egypt is limited once again if we think of it as being only a part of the whole, its scope is broadened by the greater importance of that whole. It takes its place as an integral part of Ancient History and therefore of History. It is on that basis, I believe, that Egyptology must claim its place in the intellectual economy of to-day. And the claim of History requires no advocacy from me in Cambridge.

The Herbert Thompson Professorship is a Professorship of Egyptology, and I have spoken of Egyptology in its widest possible sense, because all aspects of it are interdependent and it is essential to remember that. At the same time we have now accumulated so much knowledge on the subject that no one can attempt to be an expert in every field and specialization is becoming more and more inevitable. If without hesitation I claimed a place just now for Egyptology, it was a very modest place as that of a contributor to what I should like to call Proto-History. The specialist studies demanded of Egyptology at Cambridge, so as to overlap as little as possible with the subject at other Universities, are, as I have said, Demotic and Coptic. The purely philological importance of both has already been referred to. Historically, Demotic brings us into the classical period, and its most important material, the Ptolemaic, has undoubtedly a valuable contribution to make to the history of the Hellenistic age. Coptic, apart from its prime importance for our knowledge of Egyptian from the earliest times, has also an essentially historical function: we have yet to learn from it much more than we know at present about that peculiarly Egyptian way of religious life that provided the pattern of Western monasticism; and there are signs that our increasing understanding of the Coptic idiom and vocabulary will materially assist interpretation of Biblical texts. For both Demotic and Coptic the claims are modest enough—to be of service in wider fields.

In conclusion, I return to my starting-point. Is there room for a new Chair of Egyptology in a world which is clamouring for more and more scientists and economists? Have I the right to devote myself, and encourage others to devote themselves, to this far-off fringe of knowledge, and to leave it to the beneficent activities of biochemists to increase my expectation of life, and to the beneficent activities of economists to increase my means of livelihood? I believe the answer is yes, because, in Housman's words: 'The pursuit of knowledge, like the pursuit of righteousness, is part of man's duty to himself.'

Lightning Source UK Ltd.
Milton Keynes UK
UKHW010844131020
371488UK00001B/45

9 781107 637771